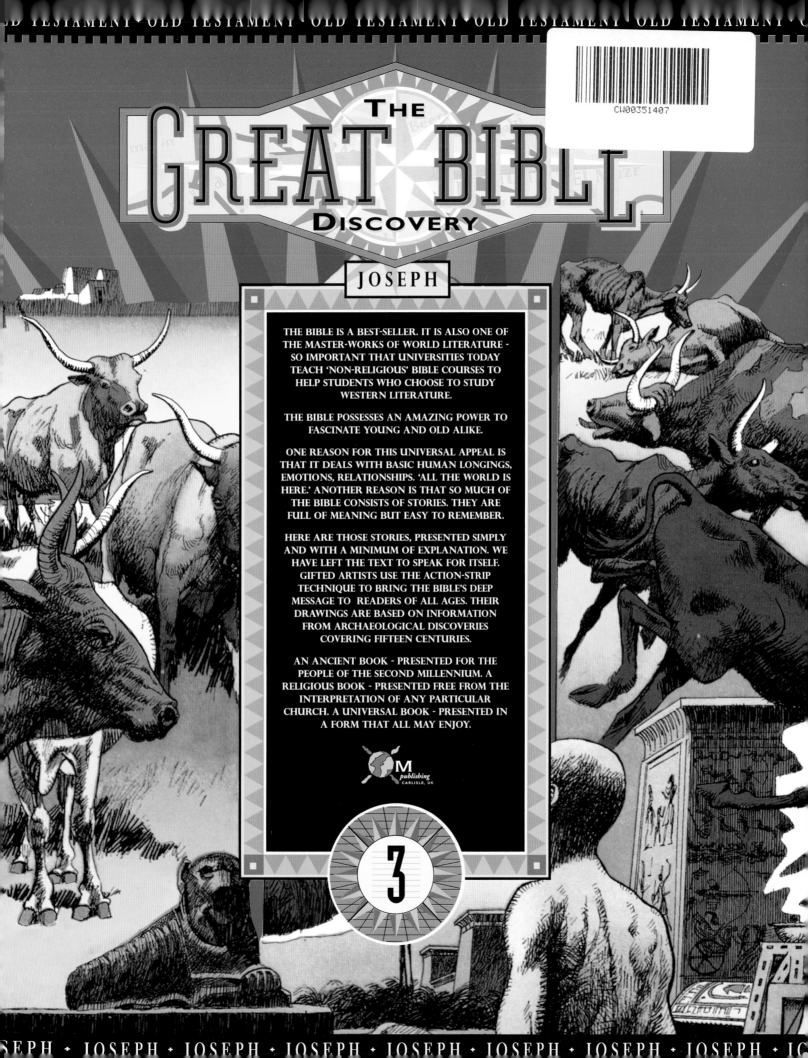

CW00351407

THE GREAT BIBLE
DISCOVERY

JOSEPH

THE BIBLE IS A BEST-SELLER. IT IS ALSO ONE OF THE MASTER-WORKS OF WORLD LITERATURE - SO IMPORTANT THAT UNIVERSITIES TODAY TEACH 'NON-RELIGIOUS' BIBLE COURSES TO HELP STUDENTS WHO CHOOSE TO STUDY WESTERN LITERATURE.

THE BIBLE POSSESSES AN AMAZING POWER TO FASCINATE YOUNG AND OLD ALIKE.

ONE REASON FOR THIS UNIVERSAL APPEAL IS THAT IT DEALS WITH BASIC HUMAN LONGINGS, EMOTIONS, RELATIONSHIPS. 'ALL THE WORLD IS HERE.' ANOTHER REASON IS THAT SO MUCH OF THE BIBLE CONSISTS OF STORIES. THEY ARE FULL OF MEANING BUT EASY TO REMEMBER.

HERE ARE THOSE STORIES, PRESENTED SIMPLY AND WITH A MINIMUM OF EXPLANATION. WE HAVE LEFT THE TEXT TO SPEAK FOR ITSELF. GIFTED ARTISTS USE THE ACTION-STRIP TECHNIQUE TO BRING THE BIBLE'S DEEP MESSAGE TO READERS OF ALL AGES. THEIR DRAWINGS ARE BASED ON INFORMATION FROM ARCHAEOLOGICAL DISCOVERIES COVERING FIFTEEN CENTURIES.

AN ANCIENT BOOK - PRESENTED FOR THE PEOPLE OF THE SECOND MILLENNIUM. A RELIGIOUS BOOK - PRESENTED FREE FROM THE INTERPRETATION OF ANY PARTICULAR CHURCH. A UNIVERSAL BOOK - PRESENTED IN A FORM THAT ALL MAY ENJOY.

M publishing
CARLISLE, UK

3

The story of Joseph is one of the most popular in the
Old Testament. It's not difficult to see why. It's about deep family
relationships, love, jealousy, hatred, reconciliation. It features a
younger son whose elder brothers ill-treat him. The
hero falls, then rises again, only to fall once more
before rising even higher. It is intensely dramatic. It
has a happy ending.

All this apart, what is it doing in the Bible? One reason is that it is
an important link in the story of the sons of Jacob or - as we more
usually say - 'the children of Israel' (for Jacob was renamed Israel
late in life). It tells how the ancestors of the twelve tribes came to
Egypt where their descendants were in the end forced to
work as slaves.

So much for the tribal history. Has the Joseph story any
deeper meaning? Certainly: it is about a brother
unjustly treated, about wrongdoers who come to
understand and openly confess that they have
done wrong, about forgiveness and reconciliation.
Any story handling such matters cannot fail to
have a 'deeper meaning'. These are powerful
themes and they touch the lives of all of us.

It is possible to go even further. Joseph himself does so,
when he tells his brother not to feel bad because "it wasn't you who
sent me here but God, in order to save your lives." The story is not
only about human relationships but about the way God works in
the world. He is able to bring good out of evil. Although what he
does may sometimes seem destructive, it is often possible at a later
date to see that he was at work to save. In this case, the 'salvation' is
extensive indeed. Egypt is saved from starvation - Jacob and his
sons likewise. The brothers are 'saved' too, for at the end of the
story they are changed characters. And if Joseph, his father's
favourite, was possibly rather objectionable at first (some people
have thought so), he too has changed by the end of the story.
He has also starred in a biblical role which will be later be re-
enacted in a variety of Old Testament theatres - that of the godly
Jew who faithfully serves a heathen monarch.

GENESIS 37-50

JOSEPH

First published as *Découvrir la Bible* 1983

First edition © Librairie Larousse 1983
English translation © Daan Retief Publishers 1990
24-volume series adaptation by Mike Jacklin © Knowledge Unlimited 1994
This edition © OM Publishing 1995

01 00 99 98 97 96 95   7 6 5 4 3 2 1

OM Publishing is an imprint of Send the Light Ltd.,
P.O. Box 300, Carlisle, Cumbria CA3 0QS, U.K.

Series editor: D. Roy Briggs
English translation: Bethan Uden
Introductions: Peter Cousins

British Library Cataloguing in Publication Data
A catalogue record for this book is available from the British Library
ISBN 1-85078-207-5

Printed in Singapore by Tien Wah Press (Pte) Ltd.

THE STORY OF JOSEPH

JOSEPH

SCENARIO : Etienne DAHLER
DRAWING : José BIELSA

JACOB
WAS A PATRIARCH IN CANAAN FOR MANY YEARS.
HE MADE HIS CAMP AT HEBRON WHERE HIS FATHER ISAAC WAS BURIED...

HE LIVED THERE WITH HIS TWELVE SONS, BORN TO HIS TWO WIVES, **LEAH** AND **RACHEL**, AND TO THEIR SERVANTS, **ZILPAH** AND **BILHAH**.

ALL THE HALF-BROTHERS QUARRELLED AMONGST THEMSELVES. REUBEN, LEAH'S ELDEST...

GAD, AND YOU, NAPHTALI, YOU'RE ONLY A SLAVE'S CHILDREN! ...OUR FATHER'S BUSINESS HAS NOTHING TO DO WITH YOU!

AND JUDAH SPOKE IN THE SAME WAY...

I'M ALSO LEAH'S SON. WHEN JACOB DIES, I'LL INHERIT MORE THAN YOU, YOU SONS OF A SLAVE!

POOR JUDAH! YOU SIX WILL HAVE TO DIVIDE UP WHAT JOSEPH'S GOOD ENOUGH TO LEAVE YOU... THAT YOUNGSTER'S THE FAVOURITE.

ONE DAY JOSEPH WAS ALONE WITH JACOB. ALL HIS BROTHERS HAD LEFT FOR SHECHEM TO LOOK AFTER THEIR FATHER'S FLOCKS.

JOSEPH!

YES, FATHER!

SON, I'M WORRIED. THERE'S NO NEWS OF YOUR BROTHERS. GO AND SEE WHAT'S HAPPENING, AND COME BACK TO TELL ME.

FOUR DAYS LATER JOSEPH ARRIVED AT SHECHEM, BUT HIS BROTHERS WERE NO LONGER THERE ...

THE SONS OF ISRAEL? THEY'VE GONE TO DOTHAN. THE HITTITES WERE PICKING A FIGHT WITH THEM.

WELL, WHAT DO YOU KNOW? SIMEON, LEVI! THE DREAMER'S COME TO VISIT US!

DON'T MISS THE CHANCE! KILL HIM! WE'LL SAY A WILD ANIMAL ATE HIM.

COME ON, THEN!

STOP! DON'T MURDER HIM! THROW HIM IN THE PIT. THEN WHAT HAPPENS TO HIM IS IN GOD'S HANDS.

BUT REUBEN WANTED TO SAVE HIS BROTHER...

LET THE SNAKES AND SCORPIONS SHARE HIM.

AAAH!

KEEP SOME FOR REUBEN.

DON'T BOTHER, JUDAH. WHAT'S HAPPENED HAS SPOILT HIS APPETITE.

ACTUALLY, REUBEN WANTED TO LEAVE HIS BROTHERS.

A LITTLE LATER...

LET'S SELL JOSEPH TO THESE MERCHANTS. HIS LIFE WILL BE SAVED AND HE WON'T BE ABLE TO HARM US...

...JUDAH SAW A CARAVAN APPROACHING...

THEY SOLD HIM FOR 20 PIECES OF SILVER TO THE MERCHANTS WHO TOOK HIM TO EGYPT.

WHEN THE MASTER HEARD HIS WIFE'S STORY, HE HAD JOSEPH ARRESTED AND FLUNG INTO THE KING'S PRISON.

HE SPENT MANY MONTHS THERE. ONE DAY HE WAS CALLED TO THE CHIEF GAOLER.

JOSEPH, I HAVEN'T HAD ANY TROUBLE WITH YOU SINCE YOU ARRIVED... YOU'RE NOT LIKE THE OTHERS...

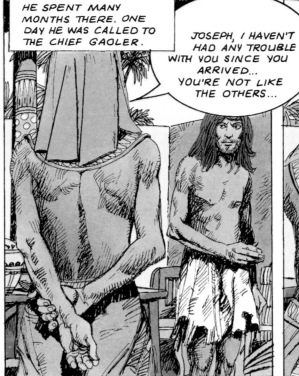

I NEED A FOREMAN... YOU'LL SEE TO THE FOOD FOR THE PRISONERS.

I'D REALLY LIKE THAT!

GRADUALLY JOSEPH ORGANIZED THE WHOLE PRISON, AND **EVERYTHING THAT HE DID WAS SUCCESSFUL.**

JOSEPH, YOU'LL TAKE CHARGE OF THOSE TWO NEW ONES. THEY'VE COME FROM THE PHARAOH'S COURT.

WHAT DID YOU DO?

WHEN I GAVE THE WINE CUP TO THE KING, BY SOME BAD LUCK A FLY HAD FALLEN INTO IT.

THE PHARAOH TOOK IT AS AN INSULT.

AS FOR ME, ONE OF MY WORKERS SIFTED THE FLOUR BADLY. SAND WAS FOUND IN THE KING'S BREAD.

I WONDER WHAT THE PHARAOH WILL DO WITH US?

ONE MORNING WHEN JOSEPH WAS GIVING THEM THEIR FOOD...

SOMETHING'S WRONG. WHAT'S HAPPENED?

WE BOTH HAD DREAMS LAST NIGHT.

AND WE CAN'T UNDERSTAND THEM.

TELL ME YOUR DREAMS. GOD WILL LET US KNOW WHAT THEY MEAN.

THE FIRST DREAM: THAT OF THE WINE STEWARD...

LISTEN TO ME! THE THREE BRANCHES ARE THREE DAYS. IN THREE DAYS THE PHARAOH WILL GIVE YOU BACK YOUR JOB.

REMEMBER ME WHEN EVERYTHING'S GOING WELL.

SPEAK TO THE PHARAOH ABOUT ME AND GET ME OUT OF THIS PRISON.

13

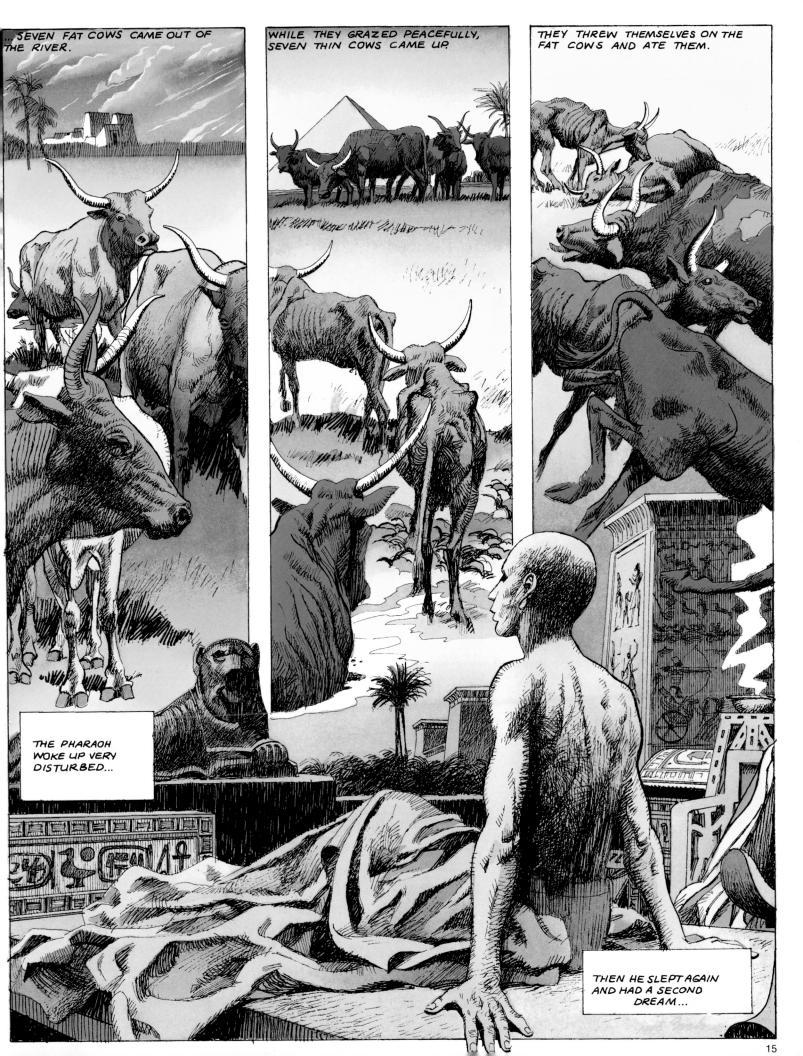

HE SAW SEVEN BIG EARS OF CORN GROWING ON ONE STALK, BUT BEHIND THEM SPROUTED SEVEN THIN, SCORCHED EARS WHICH SWALLOWED UP THE FULL ONES.

THE NEXT DAY, THE PHARAOH CALLED HIS MAGICIANS AND WISE MEN.

CAN NOBODY EXPLAIN MY DREAM?

I KNOW A HEBREW WHO MAY BE ABLE TO... BUT HE'S IN PRISON.

BRING HIM HERE AT ONCE!

IN THE OFFICE OF THE HEAD OF THE PRISON...

I HOPE YOU'RE SUCCESSFUL, JOSEPH!

HURRY UP! CUT HIS HAIR AND SHAVE HIS BEARD. THE PHARAOH'S IN ONE OF HIS MOODS.

THEN THEY DRESSED HIM IN CLOTHES FIT TO APPEAR BEFORE THE PHARAOH.

TWELVE YEARS INSIDE THOSE WALLS! I BLESS YOU, MY GOD, FOR THIS DAY I'VE LONGED FOR.

I'M LISTENING. HOW DO YOU EXPLAIN MY DREAMS?

I CAN'T DO THAT BY MYSELF. ONLY GOD HAS THE KEY TO DREAMS.

THE TWO DREAMS MEAN THE SAME THING. THERE'LL BE SEVEN YEARS OF PLENTY, THEN SEVEN YEARS OF FAMINE. THE FAMINE WILL BE SO BAD THAT IT'LL WIPE OUT THE YEARS OF PLENTY.

NOW LET THE PHARAOH CHOOSE A MAN WISE ENOUGH TO STORE UP ONE FIFTH OF THE CROPS DURING THE SEVEN YEARS OF PLENTY, SO THAT THIS COUNTRY WON'T STARVE.

YOUR GOD'S SHOWN YOU THESE THINGS. SO YOU TAKE CONTROL OF THE WHOLE LAND OF EGYPT. FROM NOW ON YOU'LL BE CALLED ZAPHENATH-PA'NEAH.*

* He who explains hidden things.

AND THE PHARAOH GAVE JOSEPH HIS ROYAL RING AND HIS GOLD CHAIN.

THEN HE GAVE HIM THE SECOND ROYAL CHARIOT.

MAKE WAY! STAND BACK!

KNEEL! KNEEL!

JOSEPH QUICKLY TOOK CHARGE OF THE COUNTRY'S CROPS.

IT LOOKS AS IF WE'LL HAVE A VERY GOOD HARVEST!

LET THE CORN BE COLLECTED IN EACH TOWN, AND GUARD IT WELL!

AND FOR SEVEN YEARS THE HARVESTS WERE GREATER THAN EVER BEFORE.

DURING THESE HAPPY TIMES, ASENATH, THE WIFE PHARAOH HAD GIVEN TO JOSEPH, BORE HIM TWO SONS, MANASSEH AND EPHRAIM.

MANASSEH

EPHRAIM

THEN, JUST AS JOSEPH HAD SAID, SEVEN YEARS OF FAMINE FOLLOWED.

JOSEPH WAS SUPERVISING THE SALE OF CORN. HE IMMEDIATELY RECOGNIZED HIS BROTHERS IN THE CROWD.

WHERE DO THESE STRANGERS COME FROM?

FROM CANAAN, MASTER.

WHERE DO YOU COME FROM?

WE'RE FROM CANAAN.

TO SPY ON US!

NO, TO BUY CORN.

THAT'S A LIE!

MINE TOO! LOOK!

MINE TOO!

IT MUST HAVE BEEN A MISTAKE. WHEN YOU GO BACK DOWN TO EGYPT, TAKE DOUBLE THE MONEY WITH YOU, AND GIVE BACK TO THE GOVERNOR WHAT WAS IN YOUR BAGS.

WEEKS PASSED. THE FAMINE GREW WORSE ALL OVER THE LAND OF CANAAN.

jové Biela

FATHER, ALL THE FOOD FROM EGYPT IS FINISHED.

GO BACK THERE!

WITHOUT BENJAMIN? THAT'S IMPOSSIBLE!

THEY WON'T SELL US A THING.

JOSEPH'S GONE, SIMEON'S GONE, AND NOW YOU WANT TO TAKE BENJAMIN AWAY FROM ME...

IF THERE'S NO OTHER WAY OUT, THEN HE MUST GO. TAKE PRESENTS FOR THIS MAN. MAY THE ALL-POWERFUL GOD PROTECT YOU. MAY HE BRING YOU ALL BACK SAFE AND SOUND.

JACOB'S SONS SET OUT FOR EGYPT AGAIN...

MASTER, THOSE YOU'VE BEEN WAITING FOR ARE BACK. THEY WANT TO SPEAK TO YOU.

LET THEM ENTER!

HOW MANY OF THEM?

TEN!

BENJAMIN MUST BE THERE!

THE STORY OF JOSEPH
JOSEPH
Part two

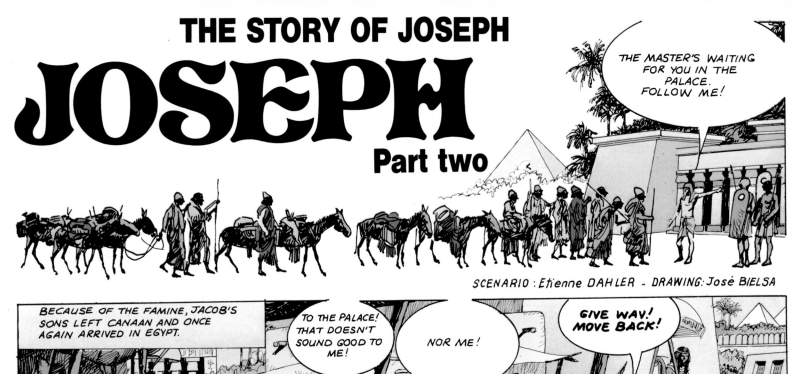

SCENARIO: Etienne DAHLER - DRAWING: José BIELSA

BECAUSE OF THE FAMINE, JACOB'S SONS LEFT CANAAN AND ONCE AGAIN ARRIVED IN EGYPT.

THE MASTER'S WAITING FOR YOU IN THE PALACE. FOLLOW ME!

TO THE PALACE! THAT DOESN'T SOUND GOOD TO ME!

NOR ME!

GIVE WAY! MOVE BACK!

WE CAME HERE SOME TIME AGO TO BUY CORN. WHEN WE GOT BACK, WE FOUND OUR MONEY.

I KNOW. YOUR GOD GAVE IT BACK TO YOU.

JOSEPH'S BROTHERS HADN'T EXPECTED TO BE TREATED LIKE THAT. THEY DIDN'T KNOW WHAT TO THINK.

DID YOU SEE THAT? THE MASTER'S HAD FOOD FROM HIS OWN TABLE TAKEN TO OUR BROTHER!

WHY PICK OUT BENJAMIN? AND HOW COULD HE SEAT US IN THIS ORDER? DOES HE KNOW OUR AGES, THEN?

THAT SAME EVENING...

THEY'RE ALL ASLEEP, MASTER.

GOOD! WHILE THEY'RE SLEEPING, THIS IS WHAT YOU MUST DO...

THE NEXT MORNING JOSEPH SENT HIS BROTHERS ON THEIR WAY WITH PLENTY OF CORN...

I DIDN'T NEED TO SUSPECT YOU. I SEE YOU'RE NOT THE SORT OF MEN TO DO WRONG.

WHEN THEY'D LEFT THE TOWN...

MASTER, I DON'T UNDERSTAND!

THEY MUST FEEL WHAT IT'S LIKE TO BE TREATED BADLY, SO THEY CAN REMEMBER...

28

I'M JOSEPH!

JOSEPH! YOUR BROTHER WHOM YOU SOLD AS A SLAVE...

DON'T FEEL BAD. IT WASN'T YOU WHO SENT ME HERE, BUT GOD, IN ORDER TO SAVE YOUR LIVES.

GO BACK TO OUR FATHER QUICKLY. TELL HIM WHAT YOU'VE SEEN AND DONE, AND BRING HIM TO EGYPT, FOR THERE'LL BE ANOTHER FIVE YEARS OF FAMINE.

BENJAMIN, MY BROTHER.

JOSEPH, FORGIVE US!

IT'S TRUE, FATHER! SEE ALL THE PROVISIONS WE'VE BROUGHT!

JOSEPH'S STILL ALIVE! THAT'S ENOUGH FOR ME. I'LL GO TO EGYPT AND SEE HIM BEFORE I DIE.

THE HEBREWS LEFT, WITH ALL THEY OWNED.

WHEN THEY ARRIVED AT BEERSHEBA, JACOB OFFERED A SACRIFICE TO THE GOD OF HIS FATHER ISAAC.

LORD, MY FATHER ISAAC NEVER LEFT THIS LAND. TODAY YOUR SERVANT HAS TO DO SO. LET YOUR WILL BE DONE.

NIGHT FELL ON THE CAMP...

JACOB! JACOB!

HERE I AM!

I AM THE LORD, THE GOD OF YOUR FATHER. DON'T BE AFRAID TO GO DOWN TO EGYPT...

AND JACOB TOOK HIS WHOLE FAMILY WITH HIM— 66 PEOPLE.

GO AHEAD, JUDAH, AND WARN JOSEPH WE'RE COMING.

WHEN THE YEARS OF FAMINE WERE OVER, EVERYTHING BEGAN TO GROW AGAIN.

WHO'D BELIEVE THIS LAND COULD PRODUCE SO MUCH!

WHAT A BLESSING!

YES, NOTHING MAKES ME WANT TO GO BACK TO CANAAN.

THE CHILDREN OF ISRAEL WERE HAPPY IN EGYPT, AND HAD MANY CHILDREN.

JACOB LIVED 17 YEARS IN EGYPT. WHEN HE FELT DEATH WAS NEAR...

JOSEPH, WHEN I'M DEAD, TAKE ME FROM EGYPT AND BURY ME IN THE TOMB OF MY FATHERS.

SWEAR IT TO ME!

I'LL DO WHAT YOU ASK. I'LL TAKE YOU BACK TO CANAAN, THE LAND GOD PROMISED TO OUR FATHER ABRAHAM.

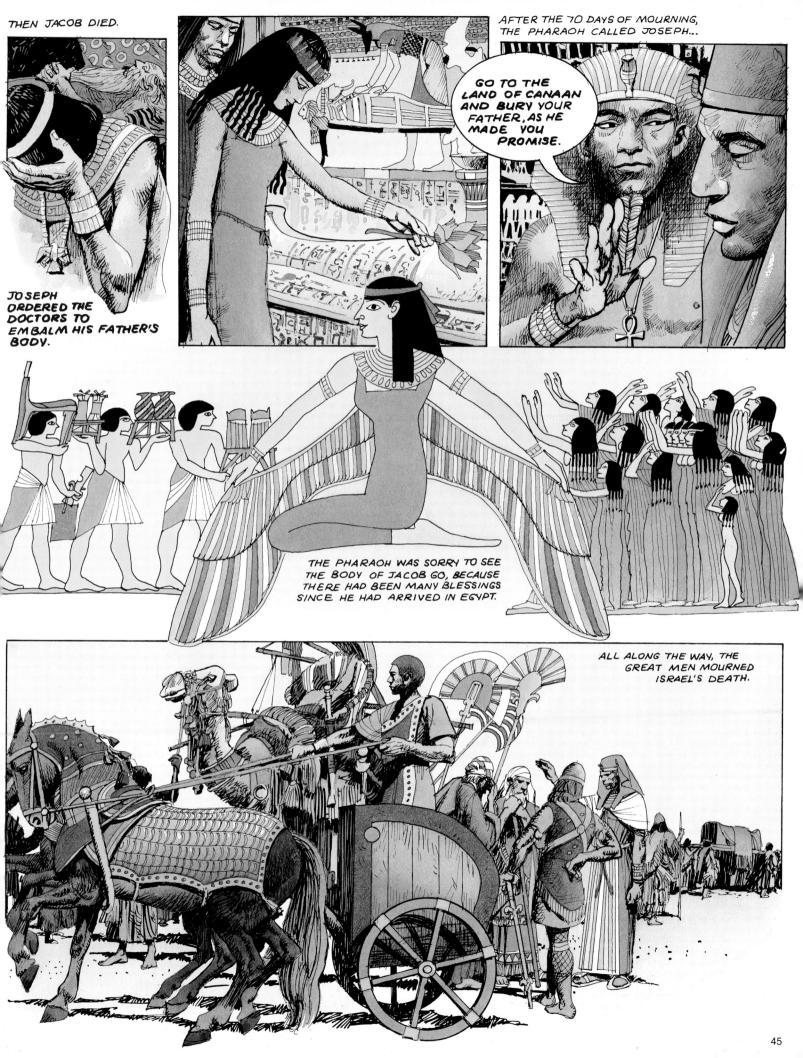

THEN JACOB DIED.

JOSEPH ORDERED THE DOCTORS TO EMBALM HIS FATHER'S BODY.

AFTER THE 70 DAYS OF MOURNING, THE PHARAOH CALLED JOSEPH...

GO TO THE LAND OF CANAAN AND BURY YOUR FATHER, AS HE MADE YOU PROMISE.

THE PHARAOH WAS SORRY TO SEE THE BODY OF JACOB GO, BECAUSE THERE HAD BEEN MANY BLESSINGS SINCE HE HAD ARRIVED IN EGYPT.

ALL ALONG THE WAY, THE GREAT MEN MOURNED ISRAEL'S DEATH.

SO JACOB JOINED HIS FATHERS, ABRAHAM AND ISAAC, AT HEBRON.

THE THREE GREAT PATRIARCHS WERE NOW TOGETHER FOR EVER.

NOW THAT THEIR FATHER WAS DEAD, THE BROTHERS FEARED THAT JOSEPH WOULD TAKE HIS REVENGE.

WHAT IF JOSEPH STILL HATES US, AND REPAYS US FOR THE WRONG WE DID HIM? JUDAH MUST SPEAK TO HIM.

JOSEPH, BEFORE HE DIED, OUR FATHER TOLD US THAT YOU MUST FORGIVE YOUR BROTHERS' CRIME.

DON'T BE AFRAID. GOD TURNED YOUR EVIL INTO GOOD, TO SAVE THE LIFE OF A GREAT NATION THROUGH WHAT HAPPENED.

THE CARAVAN WITH JOSEPH AND HIS BROTHERS RETURNED FROM CANAAN TO EGYPT.

A FEW YEARS LATER JOSEPH CALLED ALL HIS FAMILY TO A GREAT BANQUET...

THE LORD ONCE SAID TO OUR FATHER ABRAHAM; 'YOUR DESCENDANTS WILL BE STRANGERS IN A LAND NOT THEIR OWN...

... AND IN THE FOURTH GENERATION THEY'LL RETURN TO CANAAN.'

I'VE BEEN THE FIRST TO LIVE IN ANOTHER COUNTRY, BUT ALREADY I KNOW THE SONS OF MY SONS. SO THE TIME FOR THEIR RETURN MUST BE CLOSE.

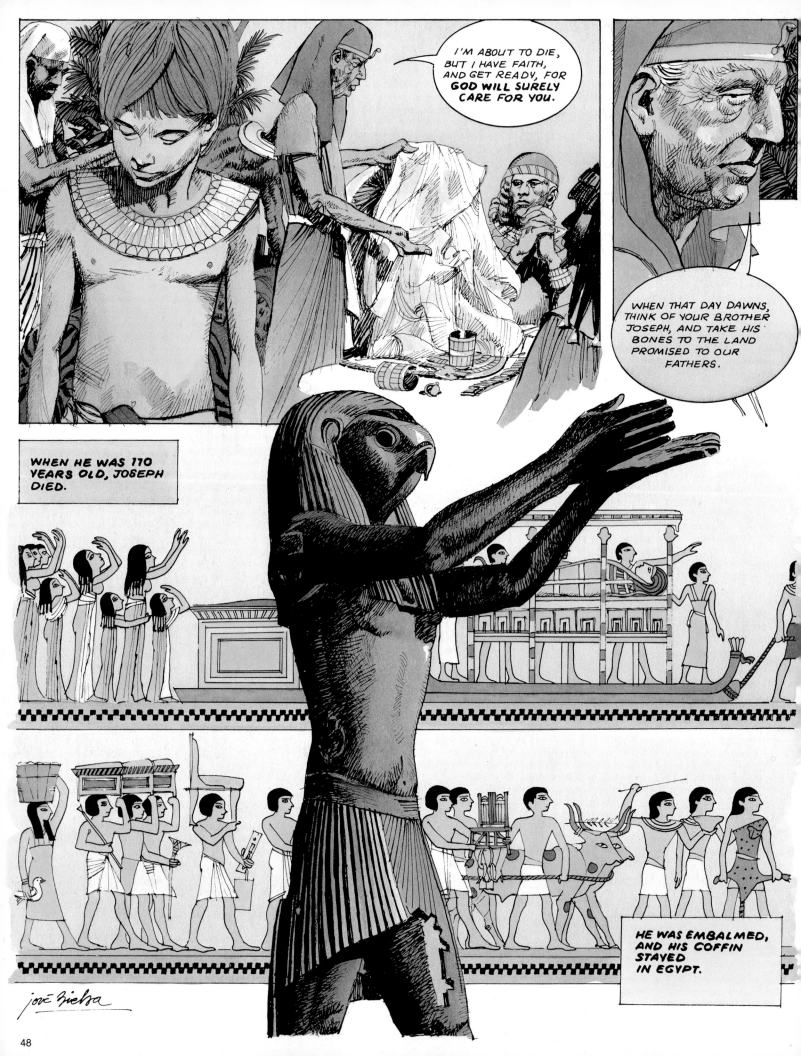